MY LOVE IS A DURIAN

UNIVERSITY OF CALGARY
Press

MY LOVE IS A DURIAN

Kelly Kaur

Brave & Brilliant Series
ISSN 2371-7238 (Print) ISSN 2371-7246 (Online)

University of Calgary Press
2500 University Drive NW
Calgary, Alberta
Canada T2N 1N4
press.ucalgary.ca

Library and Archives Canada Cataloguing in Publication

Title: My love is a durian / Kelly Kaur.
Other titles: My love is a durian (Compilation)
Names: Kaur, Kelly, author.
Series: Brave & brilliant series ; no. 50.
Description: Series statement: Brave & brilliant series ; no. 50
Identifiers: Canadiana (print) 20260175811 | Canadiana (ebook) 20260175846 | ISBN 9781773857053 (hardcover) | ISBN 9781773857060 (softcover) | ISBN 9781773857084 (PDF) | ISBN 9781773857077 (EPUB)
Subjects: LCGFT: Poetry.
Classification: LCC PS8621.A6935 M92 2026 | DDC C811/.6—dc23

The University of Calgary Press acknowledges the support of the Government of Alberta through the Alberta Media Fund for our publications. We acknowledge the financial support of the Government of Canada. We acknowledge the financial support of the Canada Council for the Arts for our publishing program.

Alberta Canada Canada Council for the Arts Conseil des Arts du Canada CERTIFIED CANADIAN PUBLISHER

The manufacturer's authorized representative in the EU for product safety is Mare Nostrum Group, B.V., Doelen 72, 4831 GR Breda, The Netherlands. Email: gpsr@mare-nostrum.co.uk

Editing by Aritha van Herk
Cover art: Colourbox #6263751
Cover design, page design, and typesetting by Melina Cusano

To Hardip Singh Bedi and Asha Kumari
(Papa and Mummy)
and Tegan and Dave

CONTENTS

SINGAPURA: LION CITY

Toa Payoh, Singapore

I have *Toa Payoh* coursing through my veins

Every silhouette of every flat etched in my psyche

The wet market between blocks 126 and 128
the pitiful death cries of roosters disrupting my peaceful sleep
every single morning
a warm carcass pungent
in my mother's basket

On the precipice of the narrow ledge of the long corridor
I polish my black National Cadet Police Corps marching boots
small circular motions

The market sweeper washes the market floor every afternoon
circular motions
a big bristle broom that whisks loudly
his shiny black rainboots rise to his knees

He glances up
waves at me

I look away

Still, I dream of marrying him
of living on clouds of love and desire
but my father's suspicious voice disrupts my Mills & Boon
    fantasy

Mother buys me a fifty cents bra from the second floor of the
    market
cheap, scratchy white cotton
with concentric circles that make my breasts strangely pointy
under my white blouse

My friends mock me
call me Madonna

The best chicken rice in Singapore beckons
on the ground floor of our HDB block
We boast like true Singaporeans

My little brother runs up and down the corridor
wearing a Kotex pad over his mouth
loops secure behind each ear
Shouts, "I'm a doctor!"

Horrified, I chase him
he creates a spectacle on the ground floor
dancing to the applause of the shop vendors

My sister, my brother, and I make yearly treks
to reminisce
about ice *kacang* balls
soya bean stalls
and homemade *kuih muih*

Happy cocoons of memory
illusionary spider webs of joy

I go back every year

Ghosts run up and down the corridor

A Singaporean Love Affair

Clandestine codes
I utter

Nasi lemak, mee rebus, mee siam
Paratha, mee pok, char kway teow,
Biryani, nasi padang, rojak, char siew pao,
Roti john, mee soto, popiah, putu piring

Embedded in my genetic taste
ravenous for the familiarity of
a sustenance
satiating
a childhood defined
a hunger usurped
a gluttonous immigrant
displaced
lost in a gumbo of new worlds
a legacy of bewilderment
longingly relishing fuel
to course through my veins

I prattle my mantra

Durian, satay, ice kacang, kaya, teh tarik
Ketupat, laksa, lontong, dosa, agar agar
Wonton mee, chili crab, fried radish cake,
Bak kut teh, chendol, gado gado

A foreigner
forever famished.

Homesick

Remember Newton Circus

Satay
Char Kway Teow
Rojak
Nasi Goreng
Murtabak
Cendol
Hainanese Chicken Rice

The soft drizzle
of the April rain?

In alien snow
temperatures below minus twenty-five
windchill factor
frostbite
icicles on
my nose hairs

All I can think of is

Roti Prata
Hokkien Mee
Nasi Lemak
Laksa
Ice Kacang
Durian

And the taste
of my accent
rich on my tongue

Hungry Ghosts, Singapore

hungry ghosts gather
roam the streets
past fiery burning bins
houses they once inhabited

smoldering pungent joss sticks
sacrificial paper cars
torched replica currency

meandering souls
trail the passageways
a promised peaceful afterlife

it's not the departed who are adrift
it's the lost living souls

patiently, I erect an altar

Hungry Ghosts Festival

I meander the skinny corridors outside my Singapore flat
sidestep fiery bins filled with pungent joss sticks
salivate over plates laden with delectable offerings
dumplings and bursting baos

Ah Soo kneels in front of her container, head bowed in quiet grief
uttering supplications for the lost soul of her beloved Ah Lim
tears cascading onto the paper money
she tosses into the fire

Peering at me through smoke and haze
her disembodied voice whispers
Uncle Lim is still wandering, lah
I must give him food and money, ok
so he can live happily with other ghosts

I nod in compassion
remembering decades of muffled screams in the night
disguised broken bones and black eyes
secret suffering

to help hungry spirit find peace in afterlife

I touch her shoulder
tenderly
exorcising ghosts of pain

Night Song

A singsong voice trills the milky horizon
artlessly punctuating the humid dusk

Om Mani Padme Hum
permeating the multicultural Singaporean darkness

Lives suspended in high rise boxes in the sky
my open window greets booming bellows
Om Mani Padme Hum

I meditate
My *Waheguru*
Your *Om gam ganapataye namaha*
Her *Alhamdulillah*
His *Blessed be thy name*

Divine love songs
ardent desires mingled and mired in earthly existence
fervent faces turned heavenwards
mortal entreaties liberated to passive clouds

Adjourn in the sky
above giant Angsana trees and
raintrees with collective canopies
braided and carefully intertwined

Your gods and mine
poised between heaven and earth

Gaudy lights cast lurid streaks
the temple nestled between the enclaves
blocks of flats
the mundane and the mystical

This piece of peace
life's beautiful narrative amid this jumble.

My Love is a Durian

My love is a durian

Furtive

Prickly, bristly, inaccessible

Takes time to comprehend

To wrench open
hidden fissures within fissures
lovingly map out the thorns
riven by invisible clefts
thrust your impatient fingers
deep into pungent flesh
nestling pale yellow, corpulence
sometimes, sweet manna
sometimes, squelchy pulpy mess
sometimes, rotten permeated mush

Prick your passionate explorations
until you whiff
how my faltering love reeks
like an unfathomable durian

PAPA

Man and Machines

Papa camouflages his frailty
his lopsided gait
fierce
proud
seeking out rails and railings to
disguise the ravages of ruthless age

Oddly nimble
ingeniously astute
he has memorized bus routes
from Bedok Reservoir to anywhere in Singapore

Once he was my unwelcome chauffeur on scooters and cars
now my eager guide on buses
yearly visits home from Canada

Every year
he repeats
his need for independence
a bicycle
his anger seethes at the unanimous silence

I find that photograph in old kitchen drawer
between skewers and brass serving spoons
my father in the back lane of Race Course Road
deftly balanced on bicycle handles
striking an angled pose
defying gravity

His sun-kissed dark hair
marbled green eyes
lopsided devilish grin
permanently captured

A Singaporean James Dean
a lion on the prowl

Time never stands still

Bicycles, scooters, motorbikes, cars
anything but a wheelchair

His mind cruises the streets of Singapore
fluid like the breeze of life

At eighty-six
he jumps onto bus 135
deft
the agility of a puma
deceptively ageless
incarnate beast

Pasar Baru, Jakarta

My sister casually pointed down the congested street we drove by,
in the heart of Pasar Baru, Jakarta

"Papa was born in one of the houses there," she said. "I don't know
which one."

I was startled,
craned my neck to see the disappearing lane of endless houses
curious
envisioning the birth of my father
in a house on that narrow street
in Java

A street with no name

In Conversation

Papa motioned to the seat on the couch

Awkwardly, I slithered next to him

He grasped my right hand
unexpectedly, clumsily

I grappled
against pulling back

Our fingers settled
in an uncomfortable truce

I leaned forward and listened
to his raspy voice
labouring
his breaths pronounced

Divulging unheard stories
lives like drifters

Sialkot, Singapore, Java
Java, Sialkot, Delhi, Singapore

Births, deaths, war, peace
a wandering nomad

Hung my head in silence
enraptured
unknown sagas

For once in my life
I simply listened

Entwined by history

Weaving

he weaves in and out of traffic
his body in unison with the machine
the Vespa purring under his loins

he becomes invincible
his helmet straps hang loose on each side
defiant of laws
believing only in the grace and movement of his machine

taking him through the back alleys of Serangoon Road
Bugis Street, Geylang, Race Course Road, Orchard Road

I clutch the handle on his seat
unwilling passenger of life

bouncing balls of fear
dancing in my belly

startled by narrow passageways
disgruntled alley passersby
shoot angry looks at his trespasses

he weaves
he contorts
he manoeuvres
like an acrobat

I flow in unison
adapt
become adept
perch perilous

cower
trepidation in my blood
anticipating
when I can jump off at my destination

our relationship
as precarious as our travails

Immigrant Daughter

our tongues diverge
separate more each passing year

unruly, unforgiving
distant continents

eyes that dim forlornly
ears that perceive silence
recollections that ebb and flow

is disenchantment caught in a vacuum of misplaced dreams?

you languish in your unforgiving armchair
hands wringing in muddled despair
strength and agility
tarnished by time
slashed by rapiers of recollection

you nod in confused comprehension

stories tumble indignantly
muddy, murky, misplaced

still, I gather each fleeting word
patiently weave eloquent tapestries
intertwined with chasms, crevasses, and cracks

your past clumsily resuscitated
your legacy permanently engraved
your history now etches
the canvas of my heart

Happy Birthday, Papa

Papa surprised

I shuffle forward
Clumsy
Dangle my arms around him
Whisper Happy Birthday in his ear

His bony breast unfurls
Awkwardly affectionate
He gently caresses my face

Have I waited this long?

To grasp and grip
In ego
In pride
In defence
In anger
In justification
In rebellion

I neglected
The complexities of love
Hidden
In the calluses
In the gaunt fingers
In the rubbles of remembrances
Waiting impatiently to be exhumed

Leaving Singapore

Papa vanishes behind
His barricade of silence

The chasm of distance
Begins to rift

Fragile connections
Careful conversations

I turn to look at him one last time
I walk out the door

The plane taxis unsteadily
In rhythm with my thoughts

The thin veil of remembrance
Intricate, flimsy nuggets of memory
Withered by age
Diminished by distance

Of man and machines
Of birthplaces unknown
Of histories unearthed
Of one more birthday
Precariously
Celebrated

All hang in balance
Together

When Death Calls

The shrill of the phone
foretells finale
every bone in my body
trembles

I walk
slowly
to the cradle
the phone jolts violently
my arms bog down,
reluctant

I know it is you
I know it is you
I know it is you

Is today a good day?

Teetering on the brink of life and death
your life perpetually
on hold
our connection quivers

I step back
and listen
callously

Until the ring tone
dies

Goodbye, Papa

I trace the contours of your absence
intricate
on the map of Singapore.

Your presence haunts me
in the most unlikely places

In a cafe on Orchard Road
unbidden cascade of grief

My tears flow into the South China Sea
your ashes kiss the sky

Sleep well, Papa
your struggle and toil are over

Rest in peace, Papa

I see you

I will always see you

Vespa Days

He sits on his Vespa outside my junior college
in the pouring rain.

The school bell rings,
the mob rushes to the edge of the canteen.

Papa holds out his hand,
palm gestures
motions me to stay in, wait
points to the angry sky.

The rain clouds will pass soon, I know.

My friend slaps me on my back.
Your Papa is here.
Mocking me.

My father
a flimsy poncho over his head and torso
soaking wet.

Perched under the corner of the jutting roof
shivering in the coldness of a typical Singapore storm.

The rain subsides.

He beckons.

Everyone waves at me
some give a standing ovation.

I am furious

At this man
at his Vespa
disturbing my college sanctuary.

Why did he come?

Today,
he floats back
on his Vespa,
simply waiting.

Dispensed with lunch to pick me up at noon,
waiting patiently while I tried to make myself invisible.

His feet in tattered slippers steady his scooter
mine in snow white Bata shoes stay dry
miss murky, muddy puddles.
I don't have the trudge down the long steep hill to the bus stop.

Today
I understand
no rainstorm could wash away my father's love.

BEDI REBELS

Marriage

arranged

under my rickety bed
in a brown suitcase with rusted brass buckles
peeled patches of leather
that heralded mummy's maiden voyage from Delhi to Singapore

silence shelters this
once wholesome
blood crimson marriage sari

mutiny shreds
fluttering ribbons in the sky

A Degree

give a woman audacity
plunk her in a classroom
watch her tongue
unfurl across continents

Rebellion

one diminutive word
          no
crumbles patriarchal chains
freedom is a Bird of Paradise

Lotus Flower

My high-pitched wails permeated the humid, grey-walled hospital
  room
Loud, angry protests
Rudely thrust into the crap of life

My mother shed bitter tears of regret
Not the son my father wanted
Coveted

A second daughter

A woman who could deliver only girl children
Useless

My mother gazed at my face
Curious scrutiny

A replica of the man, my father
She traced the handsome lines of my cheekbones
Locked eyes with my defiant gaze
And tapped my crooked, quivering nose.

My father did not show up at the hospital for two days
Only a girl
Why bother?

My grandmother dragged him to the hospital at seven p.m. on
  Saturday
Finally
Reluctant
Bitterly disappointed
Disinterested
Stood at the foot of the bed, arms folded

"Sharma, my boss, says he can adopt this girl."
His voice carried out to the main hallway

My grandmother spat on the ground
"Chi chi. This girl is the goddess, Lakshmi.
She will bring you wealth. Money. Money!"

My father snorted and marched out of the room

My mother held me to her lips and whispered in my ear
"A girl's life"

They named me *Kanwaljit*
Lotus flower
The one that grows out of crap

Did they know
I would defy the injustice of my birth?

My deafening, inconsolable cries
Reverberated around the tiny cubicle
And no one could console me

Unheard Stories

Grandmother speaks
a language
I barely understand

Leaning toward me
on her rattan bed
under the squeaky, whirring fan
hot
on a Singapore afternoon

I strain to listen
to sounds
and words
that hold no meaning for me

Wild gestures and gesticulations
urgently punctuate purpose
to an indifferent slate

I nod my head
up and down

Her tongue inaccessible

Until
we sit
in silence

Deafened by chasms of
language lost
and stories left

Forever
untold
unheard

Fresh Hot Chapatis

Mummy makes fresh chapatis

hunched in front of the flames
the cranky burner of the old kitchen stove

her arthritic eighty year-old fingers
crooked
cramped and strained
with invisible pain

her melodious evening prayers fill the tranquil air

she arches her weary back
smiles when I clap my hands in glee
fluffy chapatis
delicious dhal
spicy aloo gobi

transforms sticky gooey dough
rolled out circular rounds of raw bread
billowing ballooning rotis on the hot black tawa

I memorize
each gesture
each smile
each flicker of her eye

permanently etch this portrait
in the alcoves of my hungry soul
this tantalizing token

pure homespun love

Legacies

My grandmother tells me

her unspoiled breasts
were flat as the bridal manja she slept on
that dusky night

the one held together by jute strings
intertwined by strong arms and nimble hands
crisscrossing from frame to frame

her altar of virginity
carefully guarded *izzet*
fiercely protected
by clans, villagers, ancestors

immune to clandestine meetings in the gullies of desire
where putrid water swirled
around dainty feet in chappals

where ugly grown men groped tender mounds of breasts
behind half-erected wooden frames too small
to contain ordinary lust

their desires unfurled in a loose lungi
rearranged like bait
carelessly swirled from their waist
one big white unruly cotton column
commandeered by skilled hands
deftly folded, right over left
expertly tucked at the waist
casually primed to tumble

grandfathers, fathers, uncles, brothers, cousins, neighbours
bait gullible naïveté
young lives ensnared

girls taught stillness and silence
obedient
groomed for acquiescence
female tongues finely minced and sliced
bodies viciously caressed
callous cravings carefully contained
stories sworn to stony secrecy

men lingered in the darkness
the mouth of a child
expertly placed

my grandmother's exotic tales
swirl in the quiet nights

I judiciously nod
listen in limbo

suffocated for decades
echoed screams of compliance
subliminal old-fashioned legacies

until

when my breasts were trundled like atta
licked like an unwilling ripened mango

I heard my grandmother's voice roar
defiant

I hurled over the manja
rearranged the unpliant strings
wove my frantic uprising in complex knots

his arrogant will triumphantly restrained
his pompous voice plummeted
to a hoarse pitiful whisper

delicious, sweet mutiny

Lunar Love

The full moon tonight

mummy carries her holy arsenal on pilgrimage
to catch a glimpse of the sky's brilliance

silent in the deep night, I shadow her
diligent
seven years old, enthralled by her passion
enraptured by her magical hymns

we get off the lift at the tallest floor
of our block of flats in Toa Payoh
find a deserted corridor

I hold the round stainless steel flour sifter and laundry bat
she covers her head with her dupatta
peeks at the sky through the sieve
to avoid gazing directly at the moon
her right hand raised high
she waves her wooden bat at the moon

picks up the thali draped with silk cloth
her melodic voice breaking into devout song

homemade candles, cotton dipped in ghee
nestle in fragile clay cups
flicker unwaveringly

her silver tray laden with tiny bowls of sweets
entice

besan, barfi, gulab jamun
ardent love blazes in her eyes
unwavering faith soaked in sugared compliance

Karva Chauth she tells me
to stop my persistent interrogation

For Papa's long life

But who will fast and pray for you?
I persist

She smacks my head and whispers
here, eat barfi

I smirk at the monstrous moon
my twisted tongue coated
with sweet rebellion

Anatomy of a Widow

Singapore 1960

On the second floor of the dilapidated pre-war house
Dadiji sits at her usual spot

The lime-green kitchen table with the wobbly aluminum legs
overlooking the large window

Outside, traffic hums a slow melodic pace
between the impatient honking of harried Singaporeans
the enduring crawl of weary drivers

In the welcome coolness of the melancholic night
Dadiji peers out her window to her coveted mango tree
the one with the wild brown branches dangling
reluctant golden harvest
resplendent

With a long, bamboo *gala* for hanging laundry
permanently positioned in the corner nook beside her
she deftly dislodges the ripe curved manna
that plops onto the cement ground below
ready for its sacrifice

In the murkiness of the night
she rests, haunted by memories

No God prepares girls at thirteen
for death, demise, and destruction

Thirty years unfolded as someone's wife
now to march past her husband's pyre
a fiery existence of ambiguity
perpetual bereavement
permanently dressed in white
marked for eternity

Startled by the whispers
of unwelcome strangers in the tiny concrete compound below
she lets out a blood-curdling scream

Brazen mango thieves, foolish enough to climb
the creaky double iron gates into her sanctuary
hear the siren song of the invisible banshee
passionate bellows propelled to the bowels of earth
remonstrating and protesting the stolen bounties of life

The thieves scramble in terror
stumble raucously over the gates

Unperturbed, Dadiji rearranges her vigilance
the poise of practiced widowhood
rendered to the permanent peripheries of the living dead

Cameron Highlands, Malaysia

I dream of William Cameron stumbling upon the cool highland
 plateau in Pahang
1885, virgin, untouched land, fertile soil

Beauty neglected until 1920
when colonial transformations fashioned robust tea plantations,
rose gardens and improbable strawberry patches
rustic hill station of my childhood vacations

Papa drove hours from Singapore
up the steep, snaky road to Cameron Highlands
five of us huddled in his Toyota Corolla

We stay at the local *gurdwara* with the freezing rooms
creaking manjas, scratchy wool blankets, and putrid outdoor
 latrines

At the fragrant tea plantation
I stare at the silhouettes with baskets on their backs
movement stirs high up on the terraced hills

I float in the foggy mist,
the undulating altitudes of Tanah Rata

Calloused nimble fingers
pluck flimsy tea leaves
from the pungent bushes
on meandering paths

My basket fills
with hopes and dreams
the sweet fragrance
of tea

Steeps
my quiet rambling life

Robertson Rose Garden, Cameron Highlands

Nestled on a ten-levelled terrace hilltop
above the peaceful hills of Pahang
the garden blooms a living library of roses

colonial roots and wistful playground

I dance my childhood reveries
twirl amidst hypnotic hues
in the garden of fragrance

mesmeric scents
storm my senses
till thorns prick
my nomadic fingers

blood spills from
my rebellious heart

Revolution

ground me in rebellion
teach me to speak in tongues
forking in non-compliance

RISING UP

Canadian, Eh?

No one knows
how to be a real Canadian

Is it the coat you must wear?
put on for size
choose for type
mild cool day
buttery snowflakes
blistery blizzard
wind chill bone biting hypothermia

Back home
we simply rolled in the dark brown mud
permanently coated our psyche
to bask in the sweltering sun
sweat rivulets flowing from damp fetid armpits

no gloves, no boots, no toques, no scarves, no coats
cheap clumsy flip flops
tickling the gaps between our toes
luxurious deep green velvet grass

the surly immigration officer
holds the stamp of approval
in his hands
grudging
his eyebrows arch with misgiving
the imprint reverberates

Am I a Canadian now?

The Hyphen

I am the hyphen between east and west

one eye marvels at the peaks of the Rockies
the other gazes longingly at the Merlion

one ear hears the melodic Canadian "eh"
the other picks up the singsong Singaporean "lah"

I inhale the subtle perfume of Alberta Wild Rose
mingled with the pungent whiff of bougainvillaea

I imagine gargantuan cuts of Alberta beef
furiously dipped in satay and sambal

one leg planted firmly at the base of the Calgary Tower
the other in the bustling hub of Orchard Road

one hand immersed in frozen, icy snowbanks
the other in the tepid water of the South China Sea

I am the hesitant tourist
meandering through invisible nooks and crannies
memories embedded in far flung landscapes

I am the hyphen
divided
in the middle

two passionate lovers

embrace my tentative bisection

Understanding Perceptions

it's arduous
being brown
in a white world

sometimes I stand out
in the forest of humanity

sometimes I fade
into a landscape of dirt and mud

sometimes I am invisible
in the shroud of possibilities

sometimes I just want to be
a shade of nothing

sometimes I forget
I can be colourless

see me
for who I am

not race, colour, or creed

in understanding
love that connects us

seamless beings
of earth and sky

and everything in between

Silent Other

In my silence

You failed
to hear
the language of my
other-ness

You chose to
ignore
the wholeness inside other-ness

Silent
I othered
my other-ness
in alien landscapes
in foreign tongues
simply
to belong

Until my other-ness became
deafening existence

accepted
expected
demanded

They Are Listening

I have wandered aimlessly
through the nooks and crannies
of my lopsided house

lain on my arched back

etched histories on the ceiling
prayed fervently in the darkness
splattered words of hope
on beams defiantly
enclosing me

these walls
have ears
store shameless secrets

I zigzag
from living room to dining room
from kitchen to bedroom
tracing embedded secrets

some days
these walls

suffocate
constrict

like a madwoman
I peel layers and layers
of interrupted lives

wordlessly
erase life as I know it
erase the warm embrace of strangers
erase migration between continents

this
this is all I have

my haven is my heaven
my heaven is my haven

The Skyway

The briefest moment
when the glint of reckless sun
ricochets from the tentative bridge
of your serpentine nose
silhouetted by the pirouetting shadows
off Marina's expansive deck

Instinctively you shield
your coal black eyes
with your crooked hand

Gently place the other
on the small of my back

Trace the crumpled skin
of my disobedient neck
dampened by relentless sweat

Tenderly
you draw me in
a bewildering passionate embrace

Plant an ardent peck on the neglected
atlas of my wrinkled cheek

I raise my eyes
thirstily drink you in

Our forgotten cantilevered love
suspends

Love Struck

Love deforms my equanimity
a glazed marble statue

All these lonely years
I educated myself on the subtle arts
absorption
tyranny and trepidation

How your eyebrows upturn in perpetual consternation
How your mouth droops in dogged determination
How your hands overlap across your chest
How your voice eviscerates
How you squash mutiny

I simply asked you about this
I simply asked you about that
I simply asked

I stopped asking

Made endless offerings
at the icy altar of adoration

Until Durga manifested

Impatiently trained me in the subtle art of slaying
Mahishasura the demon

Victorious, I triumphantly left
on my loyal lion.

Birthright

Mummy sits in the corner of the room
dupatta over her head
hands in clasped obeisance
murmuring verses from the *Adi Granth*

I scream in unbearable agony
expelling this errant child from my womb

Her prayers don't make a difference
to the intense pain
but her presence in the hospital room
calms my soul

At that precise crosspoint
I envision my mother's birth

I remember my birth

I give birth

My daughter's cries fill the room
rising to a crescendo
greeting my mother's chants

Rebellious

Three generations of women
three countries
forever
inextricably linked

Rising Up

When I was born
my father placed me at the patriarchal altar
I ranted and raved. Stomped, screamed, and shouted
until my father's infinite love, reluctantly,
gave me powerful degrees, one for each hand

When my daughter was born
I breathed joy into her lips
carved words of power onto the canvas of her skin
propelled her ahead of lines of dissent
deconstructed dialogues of expectation
whispered in her ear that Barbie was too skinny
and no one needed to wear high heels unless they wanted to
let her embrace her glorious size, shape, and colour
showed her a map to female autonomy
beyond lessons learnt in classrooms and on the streets

And she became
sassy, feisty, intelligent, vivacious, beautiful, dynamic, spirited,
confident, audacious, bold, adventurous, self-sufficient, wise,
brave, broadminded, inquisitive, ambitious, savvy, liberated

We need just one advocate to

Rise up for our mothers, sisters, and daughters
Rise up for the muted and nameless
Rise up for the invisible woman

Until on her own
every single woman in the universe

Rises up for herself

Colour No Assumptions

The doctor thrusts you into my arms
Wailing and flailing
Joined by my umbilical cord

I examine every familiar limb
Trace my trembling finger on
Your smooth white, white skin
That glistens and shines
Against my lustrous cafe latte
A colour contradiction

This biology lesson forgot
My Snow White
My Snow White

There is no border
There is no race
My womb
The twain
Where worlds collide
Mingle in red, red blood
Colourless love

Prevails

The Dance of Words

I forfeited myself
at your self-proclaimed altar
too innocently
choke on my bitter, salty tears

Damn roast beef every Sunday
you shovel a chunk
of bloody steak into your gaping orifice
flourish your punctuating fork in the air

How can you not like beef?
It's good for you.
Here, eat some holy cow

At the dinner table
shameless with collected tabloid stories
of errant Canadian brown folks

At the tea party
pointing at the cheap canvas art
hanging on the walls in your basement
declaring

Look, look at these
Walmart paintings
like the loud, colourful saris
your women like to wear

Chortling at delicate Sumita's chagrin
uncomfortably folding the palla
of her lime green sari over her right shoulder
indignantly tucking it into her waist

You nonchalantly ask Dr. Mo
about Babar, the Elephant God

Dr. Mo sputters his chai
eyebrows raised in consternation
You mean Ganesh, the most revered Indian god
Lord of the Remover of Obstacles

You guffaw and reply
Yeah, Babar

Raise your cheap glass of white wine
proclaim with a smirk
You really should learn to speak
like a real Canadian
Yes. I'll get you a CB radio for Christmas
Listen and learn from our Canadian truckers
how to speak properly
Like this, eh
Tango, Tango, 10/4, good buddy
Over and out

Don't invoke the sublime
wrath of the goddess

Her tongue will slice you open
stomp on your colonial alphabet
roll out your misappropriated words
rearrange them
pulverize your patronising voice
swallow your beating heart whole
108 skulls boldly strung
on a blood-red eighteen-wheeler

Over and Out

The Justice of Death

On his deathbed
he murmurs
Can I have a real doctor
Not a foreign doctor

I stare at him
empathy expanding for his pain

His grief immeasurable
His fear insubordinate
His death imminent

There is no medicine
for ignorance

Not even looming death can colour colour

I swallow my words
let my heart magnify
beyond my colour

Compassion bids farewell
his final exit
colourless

MY Singapore Woman 2022

Inspired by a court case in Singapore where a man sued his female friend for failing to return his love and affection. Echoing "My Last Duchess" by Robert Browning, 1812-1889.

Her social media profile does no real justice
she cavorts and glances at the camera too much
dares to flash her irreverent gaze when I forbid her to continue in
    this fashion
those flirtatious looks misinterpreted; for really, they are meant
    only for me.

She brushes off my firm, loving hand on her unyielding arm

I stop her from charging out of the latest exorbitant restaurant
carefully handpicked to feed her plebian hunger
churlish ungracious woman.

What is there to comprehend?

I selected her from a million contenders for my affection
envisioned an enchanting future, an extravagant lifetime together
private condos, more than one Mercedes-Benz, mega carat
    diamonds, first-class holidays
Asia, America, Europe, the World, the Universe, the Moon, and
    the Stars.

Look, look at this extensive list of perks and promises
any wise woman would willingly yield to.

Dismissed like I was some pariah on the street corner of a dingy,
    cheap HDB flat
in the far-flung corner of this congested island

Take my business card; here, it shows who I really am
indisputable credentials.

Still, this uncharitable woman snubs the advice of my expensive
therapist
coaxing her to fathom my undying love for her

See how she averts her gaze, staring at her unremarkable palms
as if some unfaithful concubine.

I stand here like an open book; my heart entangled in passionate,
curious ways I do not resist.

Her litany of crimes is unbecoming for any woman
hard-headed obstinate, pitiable listening skills,
irrational verses that furl from her mouth
incapable of delving into any semblance of truth
playing hard to get
an unrestrained prostitute.

Incomprehensible that she dares to eradicate boundaries carefully
fashioned from
my illustrious generations

Calls for insane, despicable clauses of friendship between a man
and a woman

Unjustly stripping me of my true rights as a gentleman

Unlawfully discounting my genuine heart's desire

Plummeting me into despair and despondency

She smears my remarkable reputation with her bitter malice
Mocks me
Rips my heart into shreds of nothingness.

I am an innocent victim of my authentic, abiding love
a man of true worth and solid substance

Undeserving unrequited affection.

Come, Come.

Let the full wrath of the laws of love and just entitlement descend

Madmen, money and mayhem
douse these flames of insubordination

Permanently put in her place

Acquiescence is her rightful footstool.

Singapore Woman Speaks

These echoing collective voices
crafted and sculpted from eons of eastern sensibilities
deep-rooted roots of tradition
unheralded at birth
strangled by mothers
cursed by fathers
perpetual burdens to barter and trade
dowries despairingly accumulated
marriages hastily arranged
freedom perpetually postponed
feet bound, breasts bound, desires bound
small steps, downcast eyes, muted voice
religiously consumed by the chaste flames of funeral pyres

Deep, dark, murky heritage
invisible, subjugated, trampled
discarded, defiled, deserted
the unruly bearers of more daughters

Come, Come
Uprising is a filthy word

Our silken coats of mutiny
reckless at obstinate feet

Gaze insolently into the abyss
annihilate madmen and mayhem
rebellion and transformation
our rightful throne

The Hymen Test

She dreamt of being a police officer
lost in the muddy pathways of her sprawling *kampung*
nestled in the forgotten corners of her beautiful land
miles and miles away far from the sophisticated city of Jakarta

She prayed for miracles
for harmony in the chaos of disintegrated houses
for the promise of jobs and the dreams of possibilities
for the illusionary hope from the stars in the murky skies
for young innocent girls to walk unafraid
undisturbed and protected from intruding hands
for boisterous, unhappy, drunk men restrained
from beating their cowering wives
holding screaming babies in sarongs
huddled against mothers' quivering chests

One nineteen-year-old's dream
giving shape to dreams nested and nestled in neglected corners of
    a country
vast, unrestrained,
so invisible

She dreamt

Of her glistening police officer's uniform
Of her powerful little gun
Of her benevolent, thoughtful authority
Of her unlimited love and clout

Reluctantly, she marched to the Virginity Test Examination Room
pre-requisite for every aspiring young woman police officer

Women must uphold the integrity and morality of the nation

Twenty girls lined up
escorted in twos to dingy rooms

Undressed, she tried to hide behind confused palms
moving uncomfortably from nakedness to nakedness

Positioned anxiously on the narrow cot
two cold, unsympathetic fingers unceremoniously inserted
the questioning beam from the feeble flashlight
seeking to uncover the plight of her cryptic hymen

She arched her back to contain the excruciating pain
the unsmiling indifferent doctor

Anxiously, she waited

Only good girls can be police officers

New Beginnings

We prepare for your unforeseen journey.
Passionate prayers, rituals, rites.
Bitter jumbled chaos.
Did we forget to talk to you last week? Really talk.
Not about the weather, your friends, your family.
Ask if you are homesick.
Dismiss those aching longings for your forsaken past.
Daydream about memories of long rolling hills and scorching sun.

Promise everything will be fine in your new land.
Disgorge foreign words from twisted tongues.
Recall the aching whiff of white jasmine.

That day, we were waiting for you.
Every second, we waited patiently
While some madman ploughed your lives away.

We can't take our eyes off purposeless death.
Will you all wake, soon?
Shrouded deep in your reluctant caskets
Ironic peace and hollowness mingle.

clandestinely, we combat demons
invisible, unknown enemies
mysterious manifestoes
whittled exclusions determined by a madman's will
hatred
denying your rightful race
extinguishing the colour of your skin
silencing your fervent prayers

Hidden in the crevasses of civilized/foreign soil.
Lurking at unforeseen traffic lights.
Not time, not memories, not
Whatsoever beautiful and light
Will diminish your etchings.

We will regard every atom and molecule.
Watch every shooting star.
Listen to the shrieking wind.
Grasp icy fingers of winter's frost

Your shadows linger
In this mocking cosmos.
Sweet, sweet existence.
Bitter, bitter absence.

Eclipsing embers of hate with fiery tenderness.

Inheritance

For mothers who never sleep
For mothers who never leave
For mothers who never abdicate

When father left
carved chronicles of pain
etched wounds of rejection
onto the skin of his first-born

A child's agony discharged in
clouds of smoke
rising hopelessly
to the rafters
vacuous eyes dimmed
restless angst
in mental bayou

Unrestrained words splatter venom
blistering lesions
festering guilt

In the kitchen
she purifies
her bitter burning tears
over flames of futility
patiently

She wears his handstitched coat
pain stuffed in cavernous pockets
unruly narratives sewn into despairing hems

Absence is a bitter inheritance

My Own Skin

The five-year-old unravels at home, sobbing from assault at his
pre-school.
The proud mark of his heritage, his holy hair desecrated.
A pair of scissors in little, lethal, bully hands.
targeted. terrorized. terrified.

The teenager tastes the gritty sand of small-town Alberta.
Fists pummel his head, face, neck, torso, groin, hips, knees, shins,
ankles.
Feet kick the nooks and crannies of his twisted trunk.
Petrified,
He wears his palms like an inept shield against flailing hands and
feet.
Mocking monkey sounds infiltrate the cool April air.
No promised sanctuary.
Bruised and battered, barricaded in the prison of his fear.
they made me afraid to wear my own skin.

The polished Asian lawyer sits in his car at the corner of a busy
Vancouver boulevard.
He rolls his window down to hear the yelps of the men in the car
next to his.
Their words wallop. Slurs suspend like muck in mid-air.
His window resists the tossed bag of trash.
shame, sorrow, vulnerability.

Two young women in hijabs attacked at a park a young Black man
assaulted at the bus stop a Vietnamese woman slashed with a
knife at the mall a synagogue desecrated a Sikh man shot on
his driveway while washing his car go back to where you came
from bullets ricochet through mosques, temples, synagogues,
churches heads bowed in fervent prayer seek peace & love a
family of five Pakistanis mowed down at the traffic lights on a
serene Sunday evening by a man's shadowy truck

One lone child survives
Orphaned by hate

Still in the silence
We dream of roving ancestors
Travelling descendants' dreams
From all bends of the universe
The race for unanimity
Tender words to dress wounds
Magnificent shades and vivid tongues
Colourful hearts loving indiscriminately
Discordant minds connecting peaceably
Anthems of courage and love
Accents chanting a chorus of harmony

I am honoured to wear my own skin
I am privileged to wear my own skin
I am proud to wear my own skin
Eh

Precipice of the Periphery

cruising meandering Arizona highway a blazing summer
afternoon, music blares from worn-out speakers and floats
through unrolled windows.
tears for fears.
we chant, "Everybody wants to rule the world."
breeze from the open windows fingers my dark hair and unruly
spirals.
the cruiser takes a sharp turn, lone white police officer trails
behind.
bewilderment. trepidation. heartbeats treble.
what have we done?

"are you speeding?"
"no."
"is this rental car stolen?"
"no."
"you must be speeding?"
"hell, I said no, didn't I?"

oh my god. detention camps?

lights flicker, sirens indignant, a rude halt on a skinny shoulder of
the vast highway.

"why are you stopping us, officer?
what?
driving unsafely?
too slowly?
ok. I'll follow you to your cruiser.
here's my driver's license.
my friend? in the passenger seat? she is from Canada.
yes, she is Canadian.
yes, she has her papers.
no, she is not here looking for work.
ok. thanks for letting us go, this time.

and oh yes. thanks for the driving lesson on how to let cars in
safely on the highway.
thank you, sir."

muted. no more songs. the sky morphs into angry pockets of
darkness.

it's 2018, man, isn't it? I just want to belong.
fingerprints. thumbprints.
full frontal gaze. recorded.
and you. and you. and you. glide past my distinct invisibility.
2020. down on 17th Avenue, Calgary.
the mad and the brave venture out to sing. "Everybody wants to
rule the world."
the lovers. the haters. the clueless. masked, unruly meanderings,
crossing from one trail to the other. disconnected, I watch,
fissures of familiar anxiety from the atlas of my being.
zigzag to my origin. my mother's womb.
my gasping breaths spiral through my passports, permits, passes.
pedigree painted placards.
accents muted. the fervent marchers stomp, a raucous tempo
unfolding in ardent frenzy.
I am on the outside, eternal, infinite, perpetual outsider.
I don't want to march, join your lines of dissent, shout your songs
of protest.
I just want to belong. make no apologies. no justifications.
I stand on the precipice of the periphery.
it's 2021, man. isn't it? I just want to belong.
just like that. just like you. and you. and you. and you.
seamlessly, effortlessly, faultlessly.
no more precipices. no more peripheries.

(Y)Our Child

in the still obscurity of night
we ignored terrified whispers

stolen defenseless children
carted off by monsters, politicians, priests

sealed our fluttering eyes

saw shadows writhing in constricted cages
saw shadows wretched in man-made hell
saw shadows discarded in unmarked graves

collectively
the world
blindfolded and gagged
stood by

until one day
indignity stirred
from our lurid nightmare

the missing child
not someone else's
but seized from under our own
ever-watchful gaze

Now
(Y)Our child
Gone

Put Down Your Gun

Don't shoot my children when they are in school
when they sing "if you're happy and you know it, clap your hands"
learn how to spell C-A-T and D-O-G
wait to eat macaroni and cheese at lunch break
play tag at recess
hang out with their best friends
cower under overturned desks not meant for shields
whimper for me to protect them
startled by gunshots that fill the air

You contemptuously pound on locked doors
viciously aim your gun point blank
at quivering bellies and helpless innocence
heartbeats unwillingly stop

Don't shoot my children when they are in
church, mosque, temple, and the synagogue
heads bowed in ardent prayer
souls full of love and
in secluded sanctuary and heavenly salvation
safe with their Gods
their Priests, Prophets, and Rabbis
their spiritual journeys unending
intense devotion can't stop bullets
that sink in the crevasses of their flesh
lodge in ruptured organs not meant to explode
no faith can miraculously restore
the blood that spills on concrete floors

Don't shoot my children
when they are in bars and
move to the rhythm and beat of exhilaration
gyrate their hips and pulsating hearts
liberate their anxieties and fears

escape bigoted expectations
how they should look
who they should love
what they must be
obscure outdated rules
that denounce and destroy

let them groove
let them sway in peace
let them live their lives writing new chords
exquisite harmony

Don't you dare buy a gun

I am here to listen
show you love instead
grasp your shaking hand
hold your blistered heart
end your bitter pain

Put down your gun, my child
the time has finally come
to end the anarchy of agony

Watch me

Watch me now watch you
forever put down your gun
rail, scream, and shout
shake at the powers that be

I can't let you take away
my beautiful children's lives anymore

Sunflowers Grow

The sunflower sways in the summer breeze
tipped over a wily branch beneath the searing sun

We live our beautiful lives oceans apart

Madmen and despots rip dreams into ribbons of despair
tear tender threads held by women nurturing innocent children

Women who bid tearful goodbyes to fathers, husbands, and
brothers turned soldiers
lives redesigned for unwarranted bloodshed
callous

When summer comes, sunflowers grow
in unison, in joy, in hope, in freedom
waiting for the fateful day to bear witness
to lives, love, and land restored

A Walk by the Bow River

Rajkumari staggers from the passenger's seat of my two-door gold
mini-Renault.
Ramesh clambers out from the back.

"Ok," I make a cheerful declaration.
"Let's go for a walk."
"Phew. 30 degrees Celsius."

I wonder if my forced gusto
disguises Rajkumari's news
her terminal cancer diagnosis this morning.

Ramesh in a short-sleeved dark blue shirt and sleek, grey, silk
summer pants
A red pocket handkerchief peeks out his chest pocket
A houndstooth beret tips just so
He saunters off in regimented steps
His polished black shoes
Immediately lost in his world of ideas and philosophy.

"There he goes," protests Rajkumari.
"He has already forgotten about me. My suave Indian captain from
the British Raj army."

She hobbles on intricately bent knees and engorged feet
advanced rheumatoid arthritis.

Two cantankerous geese waddle from the water's edge to her feet.
She unleashes a genuine bellow of surprise and joy.
"Shoo, shoo," she chuckles.
She wipes tears from my cheeks and whispers,
"Death is liberty."

Growing Pains

Our footsteps echo
in uneasy unison on the tapered, slippery path
of Fish Creek Park

our breathing imprecise
words suffocated mid-gullet

apprehensive reunion
mother and son
longing to coexist
forced to seek refuge
to reconnect amidst
caving walls

the chill grasps
my usual complacency
with uneasy fingers
nature's glinting shadows
glimpsed between
soaring, striking trees

he slows down
on a steep slope
intentionally rotates his torso
to arrest my slippery foot's slide
my right hand steadies
on his left shoulder

for a fleeting, fragile moment
all is well again
all is well again
again

The Canadian Rockies

Fighting stinging tears
I trudge up
this steep Chester Lake path

He treads ahead of me
barely disguising his annoyance
seven years of steep inclines and callousness

Panting like a thirsty hound
heart palpitating furiously
I fall to the side of the narrow path
spent from the intensity within
lightheaded from the exhaustion without

He mumbles and meanders off

dismissed

again

I lie down on the moist earth
embraced by the cool, damp soil
curious hikers march past

I shrivel from shame

"Hello, there—"
A raspy disembodied voice floats
amidst the branches and trees

A mountain soul
barely sixteen
plops down on my left

"Don't worry,"
I chuckle
"I'm alive."

"Of course, you are—
the Canadian Rockies will never let you perish."

He points at a towering regal tree
long-winded story about a noisy woodpecker
another about an agitated mother black bear he fled from

My edgy breaths reach an even keel
I beam from within
the exhilaration of summer envelops me
I sit up and gaze at the peaks and valleys

He points at a soaring golden eagle
through the horizon ahead
gently presses his hand on the small of my back
stands up and ambles cheerfully down the hill

My weary heart swells
overwhelmed

kindness of the Canadian Rockies

How to Be a Writer

like a vulture
I gouge my entrails
expose ravaged skin, bright bone, raw spongy marrow
mingled in decaying dust and gritty dirt

carve illegible verses on big blank scrolls

conjure stories
intangible
insubordinate
intricate

from caves and caverns deep within
rebellious consciousness

life leaks like deep corpuscles

my marvellous manuscript
my elusive words

Hello Goodbye

Like an eternal ghost
I flit between unruly places
This boisterous world
That alien country
This familiar accent
That indigestible food
Snowstorms and fireplaces
Heatwaves and blasting air conditioners
Uncles and aunties going up lifts
Descending in elevators
Icy roads turn precarious paths
Suffocated by lingering icicles
Drowning in the South China Sea

Missing malady
A permanent immigrant's melody

ACKNOWLEDGEMENTS

I am grateful for the enduring love and endless support from my children Dave and Tegan. Thank you to my sister Nina and brother DP who always believe in me and cheer me on from Indonesia and Singapore. Special thanks to my beautiful extended family and friends in Calgary, Singapore, and around the world. Heartfelt thanks to my editor, Aritha van Herk, for her unwavering belief, encouragement, and guidance.

Some of these poems appeared in earlier form in the following anthologies, exhibitions, and periodicals:

"Women Rising Up," "Put Down Your Gun," "The Hymen Test," in North Dakota Human Rights Arts Festival, travelling exhibition.

"The Justice of Death," "My Own Skin," "Precipice of the Periphery," in the International Human Rights Art Movement, New York.

"A Singaporean Love Affair," sent to the Moon on Nova Collection of the Lunar Codex—Nova-C mission (February 2022)—and the Polaris Collection—Griffin mission (December 2025), https://www.lunarcodex.com/reading-hall-c. "Lunar Love" in Earthly edition of *The Polaris Trilogy*, Brick Street Poetry, sent to the Moon with NASA, https://www.lunarcodex.com/poetry.

"When Death Calls" in *To Let the Light In: An Anthology of Life and Death,* Sing Lit Station and the Asia Pacific Hospice Palliative Care Network.

"Marriage," "Rebellion," "A Degree," in *Roots and Wings,* Paddler Press Vol. 2.

"Lotus Flower" in Calgary Library Short Story Dispenser, Loft 112.

"Homesick" in *Sanscrit.*

"Cameron Highlands, Malaysia" in *Anak Sastra.*

"My Love is a Durian" and "Unheard Stories" in *The Best Asian Poetry 2021-22.*

"The Canadian Rockies" in *Around the World: Landscapes & Cityscapes*, Sweetycat Press.

"Hungry Ghosts, Singapore" in *The Wild Word.*

"Hungry Ghosts Festival" in *Life After Death*, ed. Tim Lindner, Tolsun Books.

BIOGRAPHY

Kelly Kaur grew up in Singapore and now lives in Calgary. Her creative works have been published around the world and beyond. Her poem, "A Singaporean's Love Affair," landed on the moon on February 22, 2024, as part of the Lunar Codex—the first historic library of its kind, declared an Artemis Accords Heritage Site. Her novel, *Letters to Singapore*, which chronicles the experiences of a newcomer to Canada, was published in 2022, and will travel to the moon on CODEX POLARIS + LunARC + ISF archives, launching to the Nobile Crater lunar region via the planned NASA CLPS-TO-20A mission.

Her poems have been exhibited in galleries and museums throughout the United States; others were choreographed and danced to by the Voices Dance Project in Ottawa. Her children's book, *Howdy, I'm Singh Hari*, the story of a pioneer Sikh rancher in Alberta, was published in 2025. She was recognized at the Alberta Legislature for her writing and for honouring Punjabi Sikh heritage for her children's book, *Howdy, I'm Singh Hari.*

An accomplished speaker, editor, and TEDx presenter, Kelly Kaur is a recipient of 2024's Top 25 Canadian Immigrant Awards. She was awarded the 2025 South Asian Inspiration Award for Outstanding Achievement in Arts and Culture.

KELLY KAUR is a writer, author, and speaker. She has been recognized at the Alberta Legislature, was awarded the South Asian Inspiration Award for Achievement in Arts and Culture, and was a recipient of the Top 25 Canadian Immigrant Award. She is the author of *Letters to Singapore* and *Howdy, I'm Singh Hari*.

BRAVE & BRILLIANT SERIES

SERIES EDITOR: Aritha van Herk, Professor Emerita, Department of English, University of Calgary

ISSN 2371-7238 (PRINT) ISSN 2371-7246 (ONLINE)

No. 1 · *The Book of Sensations* | Sheri-D Wilson
No. 2 · *Throwing the Diamond Hitch* | Emily Ursuliak
No. 3 · *Fail Safe* | Nikki Sheppy
No. 4 · *Quarry* | Tanis Franco
No. 5 · *Visible Cities* | Kathleen Wall and Veronica Geminder
No. 6 · *The Comedian* | Clem Martini
No. 7 · *The High Line Scavenger Hunt* | Lucas Crawford
No. 8 · *Exhibit* | Paul Zits
No. 9 · *Pugg's Portmanteau* | D. M. Bryan
No. 10 · *Dendrite Balconies* | Sean Braune
No. 11 · *The Red Chesterfield* | Wayne Arthurson
No. 12 · *Air Salt* | Ian Kinney
No. 13 · *Legislating Love* | Play by Natalie Meisner, with Director's Notes by Jason Mehmel, and Essays by Kevin Allen and Tereasa Maillie
No. 14 · *The Manhattan Project* | Ken Hunt
No. 15 · *Long Division* | Gil McElroy
No. 16 · *Disappearing in Reverse* | Allie McFarland
No. 17 · *Phillis* | Alison Clarke
No. 18 · *DR SAD* | David Bateman
No. 19 · *Unlocking* | Amy LeBlanc
No. 20 · *Spectral Living* | Andrea King
No. 21 · *Happy Sands* | Barb Howard
No. 22 · *In Singing, He Composed a Song* | Jeremy Stewart
No. 23 · *I Wish I Could be Peter Falk* | Paul Zits
No. 24 · *A Kid Called Chatter* | Chris Kelly
No. 25 · *the book of smaller* | rob mclennan
No. 26 · *An Orchid Astronomy* | Tasnuva Hayden
No. 27 · *Not the Apocalypse I Was Hoping For* | Leslie Greentree
No. 28 · *Refugia* | Patrick Horner
No. 29 · *Five Stalks of Grain* | Adrian Lysenko, Illustrated by Ivanka Theodosia Galadza
No. 30 · *body works* | dennis cooley
No. 31 · *East Grand Lake* | Tim Ryan
No. 32 · *Muster Points* | Lucas Crawford
No. 33 · *Flicker* | Lori Hahnel
No. 34 · *Flight Risk* | A Play by Meg Braem, with Essays by William John Pratt and by David B. Hogan and Philip D. St. John, and Director's Notes by Samantha MacDonald
No. 35 · *The Signs of No* | Judith Pond
No. 36 · *Limited Verse* | David Martin
No. 37 · *We Are Already Ghosts* | Kit Dobson
No. 38 · *Invisible Lives* | Cristalle Smith
No. 39 · *Recombinant Theory* | Joel Katelnikoff
No. 40 · *The Loom* | Andy Weaver
No. 41 · *Bonememory* | Anna Veprinska
No. 42 · *Love and War Western Style* | Rose Scollard
No. 43 · *Rag Pickers* | Blaine Newton
No. 44 · *What is Broken Binds Us* | Lorne Daniel
No. 45 · *the book of sentences* | rob mclennan
No. 46 · *We Survived Until We Could Live* | Uchechukwu Peter Umezurike
No. 47 · *Beneficiary* | JoAnn McCaig
No. 48 · *The Wiki of Babel* | Kyle Flemmer
No. 49 · *At the Freak Show* | Candas Jane Dorsey
No. 50 · *My Love is a Durian* | Kelly Kaur

www.ingramcontent.com/pod-product-compliance
Lightning Source LLC
LaVergne TN
LVHW051940300926
849280LV00033B/378